RENAL DIET

COOKBOOK FOR

BEGINNERS 2024

Delicious & Easy Recipes for Kidney
Health

DONNA E. HONG

Copyright © 2024 Donna E. Hong.

Disclaimer:

This book is intended for informational purposes only. It is not a substitute for professional medical advice, diagnosis, or treatment. Always consult with your doctor before making any changes to your diet or lifestyle, especially if you have any underlying health conditions.

TABLE OF CONTENT

Introduction:

Embracing Flavor and Health with the Renal Diet

Welcome to a culinary journey that empowers you to take charge of your kidney health! This book, your personal guide to the renal diet in 2024, is designed to transform the way you approach food – not with restriction, but with exploration and delight.

Perhaps you've recently received a diagnosis of chronic kidney disease (CKD) and feel overwhelmed by dietary adjustments. Maybe you're a concerned loved one seeking to support someone on a renal journey.

Regardless of your starting point, this book is here to bridge the gap between kidney health and delicious meals.

Let's dispel the myth that a renal diet means bland, uninspired food. We'll embark on a voyage of discovery, uncovering the hidden gems of the culinary world that not only tantalize your taste buds but also actively support your kidney function.

You'll learn about the vital role your kidneys play in keeping you healthy, and how the power of food can become a key ally in managing CKD.

This introduction serves as a roadmap for your success. We'll delve into the "whys" behind the renal diet, shedding light on the importance of managing electrolytes like sodium, potassium, and phosphorus. Fear not the science; we'll explain it in clear, easy-to-understand language.

But most importantly, we'll focus on the "how's." This book will equip you with the knowledge and tools to navigate the grocery store aisles with confidence. We'll decipher food labels, identify the best protein sources beyond traditional meats, and unlock a world of delicious low-potassium and low-phosphorus carbohydrates.

Imagine starting your day with fluffy whole-wheat pancakes bursting with juicy berries, followed by a satisfying lunch salad brimming with colorful vegetables and lean protein. Dinnertime might feature a succulent baked salmon with roasted asparagus, or a flavorful vegetarian chili packed with protein and fiber.

And who says snacks can't be healthy? We'll explore delightful options like air-popped popcorn drizzled with olive oil, or creamy yogurt with a sprinkle of berries.

This renal diet adventure is more than just about recipes – it's about empowering you to live a vibrant, flavorful life. We'll equip you with meal planning strategies and grocery shopping tips to make healthy choices a breeze. You'll discover how to navigate dining out without compromising your diet, and even find ways to adapt your culinary creations for travel and special occasions.

So, take a deep breath, and let your culinary curiosity guide you. With this book as your companion, you'll discover that the renal diet isn't just about limitations – it's about embracing delicious possibilities that nurture your body and soul. Let's get started on a journey where taste and health go hand in hand!

CHAPTER 1

Understanding the Renal Diet

The human body is a magnificent machine, and our kidneys play a crucial role in keeping it running smoothly. These bean-shaped organs, nestled on either side of your spine, act as the body's filtration system. They tirelessly work around the clock to remove waste products, excess fluids, and toxins from your blood. Imagine them as internal water treatment plants, ensuring a clean and balanced environment for your body's cells to function optimally.

However, like any machine, kidneys can experience wear and tear over time. Chronic kidney disease (CKD) is used to describe a slow loss of renal function. When CKD progresses, the kidneys become less efficient at filtering waste, leading to an accumulation of toxins and imbalances in electrolytes like sodium, potassium, and phosphorus. These imbalances can wreak havoc on your overall health, causing fatigue, high blood pressure, weak bones, and even nerve damage.

Here's where the renal diet steps in –

A strategic approach to eating that aims to support kidney function and manage these imbalances.

It's not a restrictive fad diet, but rather a mindful way of nourishing your body with the nutrients it needs while minimizing the burden on your kidneys.

Let's delve deeper into the science behind the renal diet, focusing on the key electrolytes of concern:

Sodium (Na): Table salt (sodium chloride) is a major culprit when it comes to kidney strain. Excess sodium can lead to high blood pressure, a significant risk factor for CKD progression. The renal diet emphasizes reducing sodium intake, encouraging you to read food labels carefully and opt for low-sodium alternatives.

Potassium (K): Potassium is essential for nerve and muscle function, but too much can be harmful for people with CKD. The renal diet may recommend limiting potassium-rich foods like bananas, oranges, and certain vegetables. However, it's crucial to consult a healthcare professional or registered dietitian for personalized advice, as some individuals may not need to strictly limit potassium.

Phosphorus (P): Phosphorus is vital for bone health, but in CKD, it can contribute to weak bones and vascular calcification. The renal diet often focuses on reducing phosphorus intake by limiting certain protein sources (like red meat) and dairy products.

It's important to understand that the specific restrictions of the renal diet will vary depending on the stage of your CKD and your individual needs. A healthcare professional will conduct blood tests and monitor your kidney function to create a personalized dietary plan.

But the renal diet isn't just about limitations – it's also about embracing a world of possibilities! By focusing on whole, unprocessed foods, you'll discover a treasure trove of delicious and nutritious options. We'll explore alternative protein sources beyond traditional meats, low-potassium and low-phosphorus fruits and vegetables, and healthy fats that contribute to overall well-being.

Remember, the renal diet is a journey, not a destination. With a little knowledge and the right tools, you can transform it into a source of empowerment, allowing you to take charge of your health and enjoy a flavorful, kidneyfriendly life.

Building a Foundation for Kidney-Friendly Meals

The renal diet might seem daunting at first, but fear not! In this section, we'll lay the groundwork for creating delicious and nutritious meals that support your kidney health. We'll explore the building blocks of a kidney-friendly plate, focusing on alternative protein sources, smart carbohydrate choices, and the importance of healthy fats.

Protein Powerhouses:

Protein is crucial for building and repairing tissues, and even more so for individuals with CKD. However, traditional protein sources like red meat and dairy products can be high in phosphorus, which can be detrimental for kidney function.

It's time to broaden your gastronomic experiences, then!

Here are some exciting alternatives to consider:

- Plant-Based Power: Embrace the world of beans, lentils, and peas! These protein powerhouses are packed with fiber and relatively low in phosphorus. Explore recipes for vegetarian chili, lentil soup, or hearty bean burgers.

- Fish for Thought: Fatty fish like salmon, tuna, and mackerel are excellent sources of protein and omega-3 fatty acids, which are beneficial for heart health. Enjoy baked salmon with roasted vegetables, or whip up some delicious tuna salad with chopped celery and low-fat yogurt.

- Eggs-cellent Choice: Eggs are a versatile and affordable protein source, perfect for breakfast, lunch, or dinner. Scramble them with spinach for a quick and nutritious meal, or incorporate them into omelets packed with low-potassium vegetables.

- Lean Poultry in Moderation: Chicken and turkey can still be part of the picture, but opt for lean cuts and limit portion sizes. Consider skinless, boneless chicken breasts grilled with herbs or baked turkey meatballs in a flavorful tomato sauce.

Smart Carbs:

Carbohydrates provide your body with energy, but choosing the right types is crucial for kidney health. We want to focus on complex carbohydrates that are low in potassium and phosphorus. Here are some stellar options:

- Whole Grains are Whole-Heartedly Good: Brown rice, quinoa, whole-wheat bread, and pasta are all excellent sources of complex carbs. They keep you feeling fuller for longer and provide essential dietary fiber.

- Low-Potassium Veggie Delights: Vegetables are packed with vitamins, minerals, and antioxidants. Focus on low-potassium options like green beans, bell peppers, broccoli, cauliflower, and carrots. For a tasty side dish, roast them with herbs and olive oil.

- Fruits with a Potassium Cap: While some fruits are high in potassium, there are still plenty of kidney friendly options to choose from. Opt for berries (strawberries, blueberries, and cranberries), apples, pears, and grapes. Enjoy them whole as snacks or incorporate them into yogurt parfaits.

Healthy Fats for Flavor and Function:

Don't shy away from healthy fats! Including them in your diet adds flavor and helps with satiety. Plus, certain fats are essential for nutrient absorption. Here are some hearthealthy choices:

- Olive Oil is a Liquid Gold: Extra virgin olive oil is a staple in the renal kitchen. Drizzle it on salads, use it for cooking, or incorporate it into homemade salad dressings.

- Avocados: Creamy and Nutritious: Avocados are a fantastic source of healthy fats, fiber, and potassium (in moderate amounts). Enjoy them mashed on whole-wheat toast, sliced in salads, or blended into smoothies.

- Nuts and Seeds in Moderation: Nuts and seeds offer a concentrated dose of healthy fats, protein, and fiber. However, they can also be high in phosphorus, so enjoy them in moderation. Opt for almonds, walnuts, and sunflower seeds, and be mindful of portion sizes.

By incorporating these protein powerhouses, smart carbs, and healthy fats into your meals, you'll be building a solid foundation for a delicious and kidney-friendly diet. In the next chapters, we'll explore specific recipes and meal ideas to make your culinary journey even more exciting!

CHAPTER 2

Delicious Breakfast Options for the Renal Diet:

Berry Chia Seed Pudding

(Meal Prep: 5 min, Cook Time: Overnight, Total Time: Overnight + 5 min)

Nutritional Information (per serving):

Calories: 250, Protein: 8g, Potassium: 150mg, Phosphorus: 120mg

Ingredients:

1. 1/2 cup unsweetened almond milk
2. 1/4 cup chia seeds
3. 1/4 cup mixed berries (blueberries, raspberries, strawberries)
4. 1 tablespoon plain, low-fat Greek yogurt
5. 1/2 teaspoon vanilla extract 6. Optional: Sugar substitute to taste

Steps:

- In a small jar or container, combine almond milk, chia seeds, berries, yogurt, and vanilla extract. Stir well.

- Cover and refrigerate overnight.

- In the morning, stir again before enjoying.

Scrambled Eggs with Spinach and Mushrooms

(Meal Prep: 5 min, Cook Time: 10 min, Total Time: 15 min)

Nutritional Information (per serving):

Calories: 200, Protein: 12g, Potassium: 200mg, Phosphorus: 150mg

Ingredients:

1. 2 large eggs
2. 1 cup chopped fresh spinach
3. 1/2 cup sliced mushrooms
4. 1 tablespoon olive oil
5. Salt and pepper to taste

Steps:

- Whisk the eggs in a bowl.
- In a pan set over medium heat, warm the olive oil. When the mushrooms are tender, add them and simmer for about five minutes.

- Cook the spinach for one minute, or until it has wilted.

1. Pour the egg mixture into the pan and scramble until cooked through, about 5 minutes.
2. Season with salt and pepper to taste.

Whole-Wheat Pancakes with Apple Compote

(Meal Prep: 10 min, Cook Time: 15 min, Total Time: 25 min)

Nutritional Information (per serving with 2 pancakes):

Calories: 300, Protein: 8g, Potassium: 250mg, Phosphorus: 180mg

Ingredients:

1. Pancake batter:
2. 1 cup whole-wheat flour
3. 1 teaspoon baking powder
4. 1/4 teaspoon salt

5.   1 cup unsweetened almond milk

6.   1 egg

7.   1 tablespoon melted butter

8.   1/2 teaspoon vanilla extract Apple compote:

1. 1 apple, peeled and diced

2. 1/4 cup water

3. 1 tablespoon lemon juice

4. 1/4 teaspoon ground cinnamon

5. Optional: Sugar substitute to taste

Steps:

1. For the compote, combine diced apples, water, lemon juice, and cinnamon in a small saucepan.

2. Bring to a simmer and cook until apples are softened, about 10 minutes.

3. Mash slightly with a fork. Set aside.

For the pancakes,

1. whisk together flour, baking powder, and salt in a bowl.

2. In another bowl, whisk together almond milk, egg, melted butter, and vanilla extract.

3. Combine the wet and dry ingredients until just combined. Do not overmix.

4. Heat a pan or griddle that has been gently oiled over medium heat.

5. Pour batter onto the griddle for each pancake.

6. Cook until golden brown, 2 to 3 minutes per side.

7. Serve pancakes topped with apple compote.

Breakfast Burrito with Black Beans and Scrambled Eggs

(Meal Prep: 10 min, Cook Time: 15 min, Total Time: 25 min)

Nutritional Information (per serving):

Calories: 350, Protein: 15g, Potassium: 300mg, Phosphorus: 200mg

Ingredients:

1. 1 whole-wheat tortilla
2. 1/2 cup of cooked, drained and rinsed black beans
3. 2 large eggs, scrambled
4. 1/4 cup chopped tomato
5. 1/4 cup shredded low-fat cheese (optional)
6. 1 tablespoon chopped fresh cilantro
7. Salt and pepper to taste

Steps:

1. Scramble the eggs according to recipe #2 (Scrambled Eggs with Spinach and Mushrooms).

2. Warm a whole-wheat tortilla in a dry skillet or microwave for a few seconds to make it pliable.

3. Spread the scrambled eggs evenly over the tortilla.

4. Top with black beans, chopped tomato, and cheese (if using).

5. Roll up the tortilla tightly and enjoy.

Cottage Cheese Bowl with Berries and Nuts

(Meal Prep: 5 min, Cook Time: 0 min, Total Time: 5 min)

Nutritional Information (per serving:

Calories: 200, Protein: 18g, Potassium: 220mg, Phosphorus: 180mg

Ingredients:

1. 1/2 cup low-fat cottage cheese
2. 1/2 cup mixed berries (blueberries, raspberries, strawberries)
3. 1/4 cup chopped nuts (almonds, walnuts)
4. 1 tablespoon ground flaxseed (optional)

Steps:

1. In a bowl, combine cottage cheese, berries, and nuts.
2. Sprinkle with ground flaxseed for added fiber and omega-3s (optional).
3. Enjoy!

Smoothie with Spinach, Banana, and Almond Milk

(Meal Prep: 5 min, Cook Time: 2 min, Total Time: 7 min)

Nutritional Information (per serving):

Calories: 250, Protein: 8g, Potassium: 300mg, Phosphorus: 100mg

Ingredients:

1. 1 cup unsweetened almond milk

2. 1 cup fresh spinach
3. 1/2 banana, frozen or fresh
4. 1/4 cup plain, low-fat Greek yogurt
5. 1/2 teaspoon vanilla extract
6. Ice cubes (optional)

Steps:

- In a blender, combine all ingredients and process until smooth.
- If you would like a thicker consistency, add ice cubes.

Whole-Wheat Toast with Avocado and Sliced Tomato

(Meal Prep: 5 min, Cook Time: 2 min, Total Time: 7 min)

Nutritional Information (per serving):

Calories: 200, Protein: 4g, Potassium: 400mg, Phosphorus: 80mg

Ingredients:

1. 1 slice whole-wheat toast
2. 1/4 avocado, sliced
3. 1/2 tomato, sliced
4. Salt and pepper to taste
5. Optional: Lemon juice or a balsamic vinegar drizzle

Steps:

1. Toast a slice of whole-wheat bread.
2. Mash half an avocado on the toast.
3. Top with sliced tomato.
4. Season with salt and pepper to taste.
5. Drizzle with balsamic vinegar or lemon juice for an extra flavor boost (optional).

Yogurt Parfait with Granola and Berries

(Meal Prep: 5 min, Cook Time: 0 min, Total Time: 5 min)

Nutritional Information (per serving):

Calories: 250, Protein: 10g, Potassium: 200mg, Phosphorus: 150mg

Ingredients:

1. 1/2 cup plain, low-fat Greek yogurt
2. 1/4 cup granola (choose a low-sugar option)
3. 1/2 cup mixed berries (blueberries, raspberries, strawberries)

Steps:

1. In a small glass or container, layer yogurt, granola, and berries.
2. Repeat layers for a visually appealing breakfast.
3. Enjoy!

Oatmeal with Nuts and Seeds

(Meal Prep: 5 min, Cook Time: 15 min, Total Time: 20 min)

Nutritional Information (per serving):

Calories: 300, Protein: 8g, Potassium: 200mg, Phosphorus: 180mg

Ingredients:

1. 1/2 cup rolled oats
2. 1 cup unsweetened almond milk
3. 1/4 cup chopped nuts (almonds, walnuts)
4. 1 tablespoon chia seeds
5. 1/2 teaspoon ground cinnamon
6. Optional: Sugar substitute to taste
7. Fresh berries for topping (optional)

Steps:

1. In a saucepan, combine oats, almond milk, cinnamon, and sugar substitute (if using).

2. Bring to a boil over medium heat.

3. Reduce heat and simmer for 10-15 minutes, stirring occasionally, until oats are cooked through and creamy.

4. Remove from heat and stir in chopped nuts and chia seeds.

5. Serve warm in a bowl topped with fresh berries (optional).

Whole-Wheat English Muffin with Smoked Salmon and Cream Cheese

(Meal Prep: 5 min, Cook Time: 2 min, Total Time: 7 min)

Nutritional Information (per serving):

Calories: 300, Protein: 12g, Potassium: 250mg, Phosphorus: 200mg

Ingredients:

1. 1 whole-wheat English muffin, toasted
2. 2 ounces smoked salmon
3. 2 tablespoons low-fat cream cheese
4. Fresh dill (optional)
5. Salt and pepper to taste

Steps:

1. Toast an English muffin.
2. Spread low-fat cream cheese on the toasted English muffin.
3. Top with smoked salmon slices.
4. Garnish with fresh dill (optional) and season with salt and pepper to taste.

CHAPTER 3

Delicious Lunch Options for the Renal Diet:

Tuna Salad Lettuce Wraps

(Meal Prep: 10 min, Cook Time: 0 min, Total Time: 10 min)

Nutritional Information (per serving):

Calories: 250, Protein: 20g, Potassium: 300mg, Phosphorus: 220mg

Ingredients:

1. 2 5-ounce cans of tuna apiece, packed in water and drained
2. 1/4 cup chopped celery
3. 1/4 cup chopped red onion
4. 2 tablespoons light mayonnaise
5. 1 tablespoon lemon juice
6. 1/4 teaspoon dried dill
7. Salt and pepper to taste
8. 4 large romaine lettuce leaves

Steps:

1. In a bowl, combine tuna, celery, red onion, mayonnaise, lemon juice, and dill. Season with salt and pepper to taste.
2. Wash and dry romaine lettuce leaves.
3. Fill each lettuce leaf with a scoop of tuna salad.
4. Wrap the lettuce leaves tightly and enjoy!

Chicken Caesar Salad with Homemade Dressing

(Meal Prep: 15 min, Cook Time: 15 min, Total Time: 30 min)

Nutritional Information (per serving):

Calories: 350, Protein: 25g, Potassium: 400mg, Phosphorus: 250mg

Ingredients:

1. Salad:
2. 2 grilled boneless, skinless chicken breasts, sliced
3. 2 cups romaine lettuce, chopped
4. 1/2 cup cherry tomatoes, halved
5. 1/4 cup shredded low-fat Parmesan cheese
6. Croutons (optional, choose a low-potassium option)

Dressing:

1. 1/4 cup low-fat Greek yogurt
2. 1 tablespoon olive oil
3. 1 tablespoon lemon juice
4. 1 teaspoon Dijon mustard

5. 1/4 teaspoon garlic powder

6. 1/4 teaspoon dried oregano

7. Salt and pepper to taste

Steps:

1. For the dressing, whisk together Greek yogurt, olive oil, lemon juice, Dijon mustard, garlic powder, oregano, salt, and pepper in a small bowl. Set aside.

2. Grill or bake chicken breasts according to your preference. Slice them once cooked.

3. In a large bowl, combine chopped romaine lettuce, cherry tomatoes, Parmesan cheese, and croutons (if using).

4. Top with sliced chicken breast and drizzle with homemade Caesar dressing.

Vegetarian Chili with Kidney Beans and Corn

(Meal Prep: 15 min, Cook Time: 45 min, Total Time: 1 hour)

Nutritional Information (per serving):

Calories: 300, Protein: 15g, Potassium: 450mg, Phosphorus: 280mg (Note: Potassium content can vary depending on the type of beans used)

Ingredients:

1. 1 tablespoon olive oil
2. 1 onion, chopped
3. 1 green bell pepper, chopped
4. 2 cloves garlic, minced
5. 1 teaspoon ground cumin
6. 1/2 teaspoon chili powder
7. 1/4 teaspoon smoked paprika
8. 1 (15-oz) can diced tomatoes, undrained
9. 4 cups low-sodium vegetable broth
10. 1 (15-oz) can kidney beans, rinsed and drained
11. 1 (15-oz) can black beans, rinsed and drained
12. 1 (15-oz) can corn, drained
13. Salt and pepper to taste
14. Optional toppings: Chopped fresh cilantro, low-fat shredded cheese, avocado slices

Steps:

1. In a big pot or Dutch oven, warm up the olive oil over medium heat.

2. Add onion, bell pepper, and garlic. Sauté until softened, about 5 minutes.

3. Stir in cumin, chili powder, and paprika. Cook for an additional minute.

4. Add diced tomatoes, vegetable broth, kidney beans, black beans, and corn. Bring to a boil, then reduce heat and simmer for 30 minutes, or until slightly thickened.

5. Season with salt and pepper to taste.

6. Serve hot topped with chopped fresh cilantro, lowfat shredded cheese, and avocado slices (optional).

Turkey and Vegetable Pita Pockets

(Meal Prep: 10 min, Cook Time: 15 min, Total Time: 25 min)

Nutritional Information (per serving):

Calories: 300, Protein: 20g, Potassium: 350mg, Phosphorus: 200mg

Ingredients:

1. 2 whole-wheat pita breads, warmed
2. 4 ounces sliced deli turkey breast
3. 1/2 cup chopped romaine lettuce
4. 1/4 cup sliced cucumber
5. 1/4 cup chopped tomato
6. 1/4 cup shredded carrots
7. 2 tablespoons hummus

Steps:

1. Reheat whole-wheat pita breads as directed on the package.

2. Spread hummus evenly inside each pita bread.

3. Layer with sliced turkey breast, romaine lettuce, cucumber, tomato, and shredded carrots.

4. Fold the bottom of the pita bread over the filling, then fold the sides in to create a pocket. Enjoy!

Lentil Soup with Whole-Wheat Bread

(Meal Prep: 15 min, Cook Time: 30 min, Total Time: 45 min)

Nutritional Information (per serving):

Calories: 300, Protein: 18g, Potassium: 400mg, Phosphorus: 250mg (Note: Potassium content can vary depending on the type of lentils used)

Ingredients:

1. 1 tablespoon olive oil
2. 1 onion, chopped
3. 1 carrot, chopped

4. 2 cloves garlic, minced

5. 1 teaspoon ground cumin

6. 1/2 teaspoon dried thyme

7. 4 cups low-sodium vegetable broth

8. 1 cup brown lentils, rinsed

9. 1 (14.5-oz) can diced tomatoes, undrained

10. Salt and pepper to taste

11. 2 slices whole-wheat bread, toasted (optional)

Steps:

1. In a big pot or Dutch oven, warm up the olive oil over medium heat.

2. Add onion, carrot, and garlic. Sauté until softened, about 5 minutes.

3. Stir in cumin and thyme. Cook for an additional minute.

4. Add vegetable broth, lentils, and diced tomatoes. Once the lentils are soft, bring to a boil, lower the heat, and simmer for 30 minutes.

5. Season with salt and pepper to taste.

6. Serve hot with a slice of toasted whole-wheat bread (optional).

Veggie Wrap with Low-Fat Yogurt Ranch Dip

(Meal Prep: 15 min, Cook Time: 0 min, Total Time: 15 min)

Nutritional Information (per serving):

Calories: 250, Protein: 10g, Potassium: 400mg, Phosphorus: 150mg

Ingredients:

Wrap:

1. 1 large whole-wheat tortilla
2. 1 cup mixed greens
3. 1/2 cup shredded carrots
4. 1/4 cup sliced cucumber
5. 1/4 cup chopped bell pepper
6. 2 tablespoons crumbled low-fat   feta cheese (Optional)
7. Low-fat yogurt ranch dip:
8. 1/2 cup plain, low-fat Greek yogurt
9. 1 tablespoon chopped fresh dill or chives

10. 1/2 teaspoon dried onion powder
11. 1/4 teaspoon garlic powder
12. Salt and pepper to taste

Steps:

1. For the dip, whisk together Greek yogurt, dill (or chives), onion powder, garlic powder, salt, and pepper in a small bowl. Set aside.

2. Spread a thin layer of the ranch dip on a whole-wheat tortilla.

3. Layer with mixed greens, shredded carrots, sliced cucumber, chopped bell pepper, and crumbled feta cheese (if using).

4. Roll the tortilla tightly and enjoy with the remaining yogurt ranch dip for dipping.

Leftover Chicken Salad Sandwich on Whole-Wheat Bread

(Meal Prep: 10 min, Cook Time: 0 min, Total Time: 10 min)

Nutritional Information (per serving):

Calories: 300, Protein: 20g, Potassium: 350mg, Phosphorus: 250mg (Note: Potassium content can vary depending on the type of bread used)

Ingredients:

1. 2 slices whole-wheat bread, toasted
2. 1 cup leftover grilled or baked chicken breast, chopped
3. 1/4 cup chopped celery
4. 1 tablespoon light mayonnaise
5. 1 tablespoon low-fat Greek yogurt
6. 1/4 teaspoon lemon juice
7. Salt and pepper to taste
8. Lettuce (optional)

Steps:

1. Toast two slices of whole-wheat bread.
2. In a bowl, combine chopped chicken breast, celery, mayonnaise, Greek yogurt, lemon juice, salt, and pepper.
3. Spread the chicken salad mixture on one slice of toasted bread.
4. Add lettuce (optional) for extra crunch.
5. Top with the other slice of toasted bread and enjoy!

Shrimp Scampi with Zucchini Noodles

(Meal Prep: 10 min, Cook Time: 15 min, Total Time: 25 min)

Nutritional Information (per serving):

Calories: 300, Protein: 25g, Potassium: 350mg, Phosphorus: 200mg

Ingredients:

1. 1 tablespoon olive oil
2. 2 cloves garlic, minced
3. 1/4 teaspoon red pepper flakes (optional)
4. 1/2 cup chopped cherry tomatoes
5. 1 cup cooked, deveined shrimp
6. 1/4 cup low-sodium chicken broth
7. 1 tablespoon lemon juice
8. 1/4 cup chopped fresh parsley
9. Salt and pepper to taste
10. 2 cups zucchini noodles (spiralized or julienned)

Steps:

1. In a big skillet over medium heat, warm up the olive oil.
2. Add garlic and red pepper flakes (if using). Sauté for 30 seconds, until fragrant.
3. Add cherry tomatoes and cook for 2 minutes, or until softened.
4. Stir in cooked shrimp, chicken broth, and lemon juice. Bring to a simmer and cook for 2-3 minutes, or until shrimp are heated through.
5. Season with salt and pepper to taste.
6. Meanwhile, prepare zucchini noodles according to package instructions or by spiralizing or julienning zucchini.
7. Serve shrimp scampi over zucchini noodles and garnish with chopped fresh parsley.

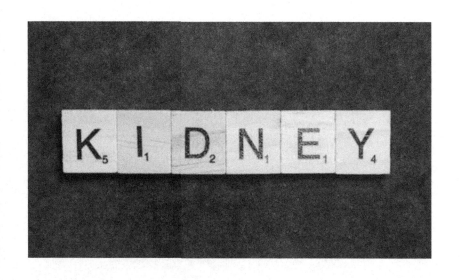

CHAPTER 4

Flavorful Dinner Options for the Renal Diet:

Baked Salmon with Lemon Herb Crust and Roasted Asparagus

(Meal Prep: 10 min, Cook Time: 20 min, Total Time: 30 min)

Nutritional Information (per serving):

Calories: 400, Protein: 30g, Potassium: 450mg,

Phosphorus: 300mg

Ingredients:

1.   2 salmon fillets (6 oz each)
2.   1 tablespoon olive oil
3.   1/4 cup chopped fresh parsley
4.   1 tablespoon dried thyme
5.   1/2 teaspoon garlic powder
6.   1/4 teaspoon paprika
7.   Salt and pepper to taste
8.   1 bunch asparagus, trimmed

Steps:

1. Preheat oven to 400°F (200°C).
2. In a small bowl, combine olive oil, parsley, thyme, garlic powder, paprika, salt, and pepper.
3. Arrange the salmon fillets on a parchment paper lined baking pan..
4. Spread the herb mixture evenly over the top of each salmon fillet.
5. Add a little olive oil to the asparagus and toss to coat, then season with salt and pepper. Arrange the asparagus alongside the salmon on the baking sheet.
6. Bake for 15-20 minutes, or until salmon is cooked through and flakes easily with a fork.

Turkey Chili with Brown Rice

(Meal Prep: 15 min, Cook Time: 45 min, Total Time: 1 hour)

Nutritional Information (per serving):

Calories: 450, Protein: 30g, Potassium: 500mg, Phosphorus: 350mg (Note: Potassium content can vary depending on the type of beans used)

Ingredients:

1. 1 tablespoon olive oil
2. 1 onion, chopped
3. 1 green bell pepper, chopped
4. 2 cloves garlic, minced
5. 1 teaspoon ground cumin
6. 1/2 teaspoon chili powder
7. 1/4 teaspoon smoked paprika
8. 1 (15-oz) can diced tomatoes, undrained
9. 4 cups low-sodium vegetable broth
10. 1 pound ground turkey
11. 1 (15-oz) can kidney beans, rinsed and drained
12. 1 (15-oz) can black beans, rinsed and drained
13. 1 cup cooked brown rice

14. Salt and pepper to taste
15. Optional toppings: Chopped fresh cilantro, low-fat shredded cheese, avocado slices

Steps:

1. In a big pot or Dutch oven, warm up the olive oil over medium heat.
2. Add onion, bell pepper, and garlic. Sauté until softened, about 5 minutes.
3. Stir in cumin, chili powder, and paprika. Cook for an additional minute.
4. Add diced tomatoes, vegetable broth, ground turkey, kidney beans, and black beans. Bring to a boil, then reduce heat and simmer for 30 minutes, or until slightly thickened.
5. Stir in cooked brown rice. Season with salt and pepper to taste.
6. Serve hot topped with chopped fresh cilantro, lowfat shredded cheese, and avocado slices (optional).

Chicken Stir-Fry with Vegetables and Brown Rice

(Meal Prep: 15 min, Cook Time: 20 min, Total Time: 35 min)

Nutritional Information (per serving):

Calories: 400, Protein: 35g, Potassium: 550mg, Phosphorus: 300mg **Ingredients:**

1. 1 tablespoon olive oil
2. 1 pound boneless, skinless chicken breasts, sliced
3. 1 cup broccoli florets
4. 1 cup sliced red bell pepper
5. 1/2 cup chopped carrots

6. 1/4 cup low-sodium soy sauce
7. 2 tablespoons cornstarch
8. 1 tablespoon rice vinegar
9. 1 teaspoon grated ginger
10. 1/2 teaspoon garlic powder
11. 1 cup cooked brown rice

Steps:

1. In a small bowl, whisk together soy sauce, cornstarch, rice vinegar, ginger, and garlic powder. Set aside.
2. In a large skillet or wok, heat the olive oil over medium-high heat.
3. Cook the chicken for five to seven minutes, or until it is thoroughly cooked and browned.
4. Stir in broccoli, red bell pepper, and carrots. Cook the vegetables for a further five minutes, or until they are crisp-tender.
5. After adding the soy sauce mixture to the pan, simmer it. Simmer for one to two minutes, or until the sauce begins to slightly thicken.
6. Serve stir-fry over cooked brown rice.

Vegetarian Stuffed Peppers with Quinoa

(Meal Prep: 15 min, Cook Time: 45 min, Total Time: 1 hour)

Nutritional Information (per serving):

Calories: 400, Protein: 15g, Potassium: 500mg, Phosphorus: 250mg

Ingredients:

1. 4 bell peppers (red, yellow, orange, or green)
2. 1 tablespoon olive oil
3. 1 onion, chopped
4. 1 clove garlic, minced
5. 1 cup cooked quinoa
6. 1 (15-oz) can black beans, rinsed and drained
7. 1 (14.5-oz) can diced tomatoes, undrained
8. 1/2 cup chopped corn
9. 1/4 cup chopped fresh cilantro
10. 1 teaspoon ground cumin
11. 1/2 teaspoon chili powder
12. Salt and pepper to taste
13. 1/4 cup shredded low-fat cheese (optional)

Steps:

1. Preheat oven to 375°F (190°C).
2. Slice off the bell peppers' tops, then take out the seeds and membranes. Rinse and pat dry.
3. In a big skillet over medium heat, warm up the olive oil.
4. Add onion and garlic. Sauté until softened, about 5 minutes.
5. Stir in cooked quinoa, black beans, diced tomatoes, corn, cilantro, cumin, and chili powder. Season with salt and pepper to taste.
6. Filling mixture should be spooned into prepared bell peppers. Top with shredded cheese (if using).
7. Place bell peppers in a baking dish and bake for 3035 minutes, or until peppers are tender and filling is heated through.

Baked Cod with Lemon Dill Sauce and Roasted Brussels Sprouts

(Meal Prep: 10 min, Cook Time: 20 min, Total Time: 30 min)

Nutritional Information (per serving):

Calories: 350, Protein: 30g, Potassium: 400mg, Phosphorus: 250mg

Ingredients:

1. 2 cod fillets (6 oz each)
2. 1 tablespoon olive oil
3. 1/4 cup chopped fresh dill
4. 1 tablespoon lemon juice
5. 1/2 teaspoon garlic powder
6. Salt and pepper to taste
7. 1 pound Brussels sprouts, trimmed and halved

Steps:

1. Preheat oven to 400°F (200°C).
2. In a small bowl, whisk together olive oil, dill, lemon juice, and garlic powder.
3. Cod fillets should be placed on a baking pan covered with parchment paper.
4. Brush the lemon dill sauce evenly over the top of each cod fillet.
5. Season with salt and pepper to taste.
6. After drizzling some olive oil over the Brussels sprouts, add some salt and pepper to taste. Arrange the Brussels sprouts alongside the cod fillets on the baking sheet.
7. Bake for 15-20 minutes, or until cod is cooked through and flakes easily with a fork and Brussels sprouts are tender-crisp.

Lemon Garlic Shrimp with Whole-Wheat Pasta

(Meal Prep: 10 min, Cook Time: 15 min, Total Time: 25 min)

Nutritional Information (per serving):

Calories: 400, Protein: 30g, Potassium: 450mg, Phosphorus: 320mg (Note: Potassium content can vary depending on the type of pasta used)

Ingredients:

1. 1 tablespoon olive oil
2. 2 cloves garlic, minced
3. 1/2 teaspoon red pepper flakes (optional)
4. 1 cup cherry tomatoes, halved
5. 1 pound deveined shrimp, peeled and tails removed (if desired)
6. 1/4 cup low-sodium chicken broth
7. 1 tablespoon lemon juice
8. 1/4 cup chopped fresh parsley
9. Salt and pepper to taste
10. 2 cups cooked whole-wheat pasta

Steps:

1. Cook whole-wheat pasta according to package instructions. Drain and set aside.
2. In a big skillet over medium heat, warm up the olive oil.
3. Add garlic and red pepper flakes (if using). Sauté for 30 seconds, until fragrant.
4. Add cherry tomatoes and cook for 2 minutes, or until softened and starting to burst.
5. Stir in shrimp, chicken broth, and lemon juice. Bring to a simmer and cook for 3-5 minutes, or until shrimp are pink and cooked through.
6. Season with salt and pepper to taste.
7. Toss cooked pasta with the shrimp and sauce. Garnish with chopped fresh parsley.

Vegetarian Black Bean Burgers with Sweet Potato Fries

(Meal Prep: 15 min, Cook Time: 20 min, Total Time: 35 min)

Nutritional Information (per serving):

Calories: 400, Protein: 18g, Potassium: 500mg, Phosphorus: 300mg

Ingredients:

1. Black bean burgers:
2. 1 (15-oz) can black beans, rinsed and drained
3. 1/2 cup cooked brown rice
4. 1/4 cup chopped onion
5. 1/4 cup chopped red bell pepper

6. 1 tablespoon chopped fresh cilantro
7. 1 tablespoon olive oil
8. 1 egg, beaten (optional)
9. 1/2 teaspoon ground cumin
10. 1/4 teaspoon chili powder 11. Salt and pepper to taste
    12.   Sweet potato fries:
    13.   2 sweet potatoes, cut into wedges
    14.   1 tablespoon olive oil
    15.   1/2 teaspoon paprika
    16.   Salt and pepper to taste

Steps:

1. Preheat oven to 400°F (200°C).
2. For the sweet potato fries, toss sweet potato wedges with olive oil, paprika, salt, and pepper. Spread on a baking sheet and bake for 20-25 minutes, or until tender and golden brown, flipping halfway through.
3. Mash the black beans with a fork in a big bowl. Stir in cooked brown rice, onion, red bell pepper, cilantro, olive oil, egg (if using), cumin, chili powder, salt, and pepper.
4. Form the mixture into burger patties.
5. Heat a large skillet over medium heat. The black bean burgers should be cooked for 4–5 minutes on each side, or until well-done and thoroughly heated. 6. Serve black bean burgers on hamburger buns (optional) with your favorite toppings and sweet potato fries on the side.

Chicken Fajitas with Whole-Wheat Tortillas

(Meal Prep: 15 min, Cook Time: 20 min, Total Time: 35 min)

Nutritional Information (per serving):

Calories: 450, Protein: 40g, Potassium: 500 mg, Phosphorus: 350mg

Ingredients:

1. 1 tablespoon olive oil
2. 1 pound boneless, skinless chicken breasts, sliced
3. 1 onion, sliced
4. 1 green bell pepper, sliced
5. 1 red bell pepper, sliced
6. 1 teaspoon ground cumin
7. 1/2 teaspoon chili powder
8. 1/4 teaspoon smoked paprika
9. Salt and pepper to taste
10. 4 whole-wheat tortillas
11. Optional toppings: Chopped lettuce, sliced avocado, low-fat shredded cheese, salsa, low-fat Greek yogurt

Steps:

1. In a large skillet or grill pan, heat the olive oil over medium-high heat.
2. Cook the chicken for five to seven minutes, or until it is thoroughly cooked and browned.
3. Take out and set aside the chicken from the pan.
4. Add onion, green bell pepper, and red bell pepper to the pan. Sauté for 5-7 minutes, or until softened and slightly browned.
5. Stir in cumin, chili powder, and paprika. Season with salt and pepper to taste.
6. Warm whole-wheat tortillas according to package instructions.
7. Serve chicken and fajita vegetables on warmed tortillas. Let everyone customize their fajitas with their favorite toppings like chopped lettuce, sliced avocado, low-fat shredded cheese, salsa, or low-fat Greek yogurt.

One-Pan Lemon Herb Salmon with Roasted Asparagus and Quinoa

(Meal Prep: 10 min, Cook Time: 20 min, Total Time: 30 min)

Nutritional Information (per serving):

Calories: 400, Protein: 35g, Potassium: 450mg, Phosphorus: 320mg

Ingredients:

1. 2 salmon fillets (6 oz each)
2. 1 tablespoon olive oil
3. 1/4 cup chopped fresh parsley
4. 1 tablespoon dried thyme
5. 1/2 teaspoon garlic powder
6. 1/4 teaspoon paprika
7. Salt and pepper to taste
8. 1 cup quinoa, rinsed
9. 1 1/2 cups low-sodium vegetable broth
10. 1 bunch asparagus, trimmed
11.

Steps:

1. Preheat oven to 400°F (200°C).
2. In a small bowl, combine olive oil, parsley, thyme, garlic powder, paprika, salt, and pepper.
3. Put the salmon fillets on a baking sheet with a rim.
4. Spread the herb mixture evenly over the top of each salmon fillet.
5. Rinse quinoa and add it to the baking sheet around the salmon. Pour in vegetable broth.
6. Add a little olive oil to the asparagus and toss to coat, then season with salt and pepper. Arrange the asparagus alongside the salmon and quinoa on the baking sheet.
7. Bake for 15-20 minutes, or until salmon is cooked through and flakes easily with a fork, quinoa is cooked through and fluffy, and asparagus is tender crisp.

Vegetarian Lentil Soup with Crusty Bread

(Meal Prep: 15 min, Cook Time: 45 min, Total Time: 1 hour)

Nutritional Information (per serving):

Calories: 350, Protein: 18g, Potassium: 500mg, Phosphorus: 280mg (Note: Potassium content can vary depending on the type of lentils used)

Ingredients:

1. 1 tablespoon olive oil
2. 1 onion, chopped
3. 1 carrot, chopped
4. 2 cloves garlic, minced
5. 1 teaspoon ground cumin
6. 1/2 teaspoon dried thyme
7. 4 cups low-sodium vegetable broth
8. 1 cup brown lentils, rinsed
9. 1 (14.5-oz) can diced tomatoes, undrained
10. Salt and pepper to taste

11. Crusty bread for serving (optional)

Steps:

1. In a big pot or Dutch oven, warm up the olive oil over medium heat.

2. Add onion, carrot, and garlic. Sauté until softened, about 5 minutes.

3. Stir in cumin and thyme. Cook for an additional minute.

4. Add vegetable broth, lentils, and diced tomatoes. Bring to a boil, then reduce heat and simmer for 3035 minutes, or until lentils are tender.

5. Season with salt and pepper to taste.

6. Serve hot with a slice of crusty bread for dipping (optional).

CHAPTER 5

Healthy Kidney-Friendly Snacks for Everyone to Enjoy: Edamame with Sea Salt

(Meal Prep Time: 5 min, Cook Time: 3-5 min, Total Time: 8 min)

Nutritional Information (per serving, ½ cup cooked edamame)

Calories: 120, Protein: 12g, Potassium: 170mg, Phosphorus: 140mg

Ingredients:

1. 1 cup frozen shelled edamame
2. Sea salt, to taste

Steps:

1. In a pot, bring the water to a boil.
2. Add frozen edamame and cook for 3-5 minutes, or according to package instructions.
3. Drain and rinse with cold water.
4. Sprinkle with sea salt to taste.

Greek Yogurt with Berries and Sliced Almonds

(Meal Prep Time: 2 min, Cook Time: 0 min, Total Time: 2 min)

Nutritional Information (per serving, 1 cup plain Greek yogurt ½ cup berries, ¼ cup sliced almonds):

Calories: 300, Protein: 20g, Potassium: 350mg, Phosphorus: 200mg

Ingredients:

1. 1 cup plain Greek yogurt (2% or low-fat)
2. ½ cup fresh or frozen berries (blueberries, raspberries, strawberries)
3. ¼ cup sliced almonds

Steps:

1. In a bowl, combine Greek yogurt, berries, and sliced almonds.
2. Stir gently and enjoy!

Apple Slices with Cinnamon Peanut Butter

(Meal Prep Time: 2 min, Cook Time: 0 min, Total Time: 2 min)

Nutritional Information (per serving, 1 apple, 2 tbsp peanut butter):

Calories: 300, Protein: 8g, Potassium: 200mg, Phosphorus: 180mg

Ingredients:

1. 1 apple, sliced
2. 2 tablespoons peanut butter (consider natural peanut butter for lower sodium content)

Steps:

1. Slice an apple into wedges or desired shapes.
2. Spread peanut butter on apple slices.

Cottage Cheese with Chopped Vegetables and Herbs

(Meal Prep Time: 5 min, Cook Time: 0 min, Total Time: 5 min)

Nutritional Information (per serving, ½ cup cottage cheese, ¼ cup chopped vegetables, 1 tbsp chopped herbs):

Calories: 150, Protein: 15g, Potassium: 220mg, Phosphorus: 150mg

Ingredients:

1. ½ cup low-fat cottage cheese
2. ¼ cup chopped vegetables (cucumber, bell pepper, cherry tomatoes)
3. 1 tablespoon chopped fresh herbs (dill, chives, parsley)

Steps:

1. In a bowl, combine cottage cheese, chopped vegetables, and chopped herbs.
2. Stir gently and enjoy!

Rice Cakes with Avocado and Sliced Tomatoes

(Meal Prep Time: 2 min, Cook Time: 0 min, Total Time: 2 min)

Nutritional Information (per serving, 2 rice cakes, ¼ avocado, 1 sliced tomato):

Calories: 200, Protein: 2g, Potassium: 300mg, Phosphorus: 80mg

Ingredients:

1. 2 brown rice cakes
2. ¼ avocado, sliced
3. 1 tomato, sliced

Steps:

1. Spread avocado slices on rice cakes.
2. Top with sliced tomato.

Carrot Sticks with Hummus

(Meal Prep Time: 2 min, Cook Time: 0 min, Total Time: 2 min)

Nutritional Information (per serving, 1 cup baby carrots, 3 tbsp hummus):

Calories: 250, Protein: 6g, Potassium: 450mg, Phosphorus: 170mg

Ingredients:

1. 1 cup baby carrots
2. 3 tablespoons hummus (consider low-sodium options)

Steps:

1. Wash and prepare baby carrots.
2. Serve with hummus for dipping.

Homemade Trail Mix

(Meal Prep Time: 10 min, Cook Time: 0 min, Total Time: 10 min)

Nutritional Information (per serving, ½ cup trail mix - customize based on ingredients):

Calories: 250 (varies), Protein: 10g (varies), Potassium: 200mg (varies), Phosphorus: 150mg (varies)

Ingredients:

1. 1/4 cup dry cereal (choose low-sugar options like Cheerios or bran flakes)

2. 1/4 cup unsalted nuts (almonds, walnuts, cashews)

3. 1/4 cup dried fruit (cranberries, raisins, cherries)

4. 1/4 cup roasted chickpeas (optional)

5. Additional options: shredded coconut (unsweetened), dark chocolate chips (limited quantity)

Steps:

1. In a bowl, combine dry cereal, nuts, dried fruit, and any additional chosen ingredients.

2. Mix well and store in an airtight container for up to a week.

Bell Pepper Slices with Guacamole

(Meal Prep Time: 5 min, Cook Time: 0 min, Total Time: 5 min)

Nutritional Information (per serving, 1 bell pepper, ¼ cup guacamole):

Calories: 150, Protein: 2g, Potassium: 350mg, Phosphorus: 80mg

Ingredients:

1. 1 bell pepper (red, yellow, orange, or green), sliced
2. ¼ cup guacamole (consider making your own with fresh avocado, lime juice, and spices for lower sodium content)

Steps:

1. Slice bell pepper into strips or desired shapes.
2. Serve with guacamole for dipping.

Air-Popped Popcorn with Nutritional Yeast

(Meal Prep Time: 5 min, Cook Time: 5 min, Total Time: 10 min

Nutritional Information (per serving, 3 cups air-popped popcorn, 2 tbsp nutritional yeast):

Calories: 150, Protein: 5g, Potassium: 100mg, Phosphorus: 120mg

Ingredients:

1. 3 tablespoons popcorn kernels
2. 2 tablespoons nutritional yeast

Steps:

1. Air-pop popcorn according to your air popper's instructions.
2. Sprinkle nutritional yeast over popcorn and toss to coat.

Hard-Boiled Eggs

(Meal Prep Time: 10 min, Cook Time: 12-15 min, Total Time: 22-25 min)

Nutritional Information (per serving, 1 large hard-boiled egg):

Calories: 78, Protein: 6g, Potassium: 78mg, Phosphorus: 91mg

Ingredients:

1. Eggs (quantity depends on how many you want to prepare) **Steps:**

2. Put the eggs in a saucepan in a single layer.
3. Pour cold water over eggs and bring to a boil.
4. Once boiling, remove from heat, cover, and let sit for 12-15 minutes.
5. Drain hot water and rinse eggs with cold water until cool enough to handle.
6. Peel and enjoy!

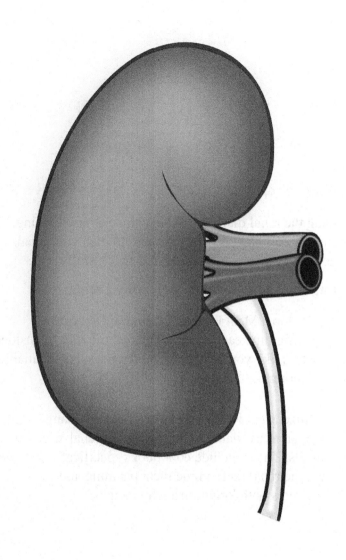

CHAPTER 6

Living Well with the Renal Diet Meal Planning & Grocery Shopping: Success Strategies

Following the renal diet doesn't have to be overwhelming. This chapter equips you with strategies to plan your meals and shop for groceries efficiently and successfully.

Planning Ahead for a Week of Healthy Eating:

- Develop a Meal Planning Routine: Dedicate a specific time each week to plan your meals. Consider factors like your schedule, preferences, and available ingredients.

- Utilize Meal Planning Tools: There are many resources available to help you plan renal-friendly meals. These include cookbooks specifically designed for the renal diet, online meal planning apps, and websites with kidney-friendly recipes.

- Create a Template: Develop a basic template for your week's meals, including breakfast, lunch, dinner, and snacks. This helps ensure variety and reduces the daily decision fatigue.

- Consider Leftovers: Plan meals with leftovers in mind. Leftovers can be repurposed for lunch the next day or creatively incorporated into new dishes.

- Involve the Family: Planning meals together can be a fun and educational activity. It allows you to explore new recipes as a family and ensure everyone enjoys the meals.

Smart Shopping on a Budget:

- Make a Shopping List: Sticking to a list helps you avoid impulse purchases that might not be renalfriendly. Include all the ingredients you need for your planned meals and snacks.

- Shop in Season: Seasonal produce is typically fresher, more affordable, and often has a better taste.

- Buy in Bulk (Smartly): Purchasing staples like whole grains, canned beans, and frozen vegetables in bulk can save money in the long run. However, only buy in bulk if you have the storage space and will use the ingredients before they expire.

- Compare Prices and Look for Deals: Check unit prices and flyers for promotions on renal-friendly options. Utilize store loyalty programs and coupons for additional savings.

- :Take a Look at Generic Brands: These brands frequently provide name brands' quality at a lesser price. Compare the ingredients list and nutrition information to ensure suitability for your diet.

- Plan Around Sales: Plan your meals around grocery store sales flyers and stock up on discounted staples when possible.

- Minimize Food Waste: Proper storage and meal planning can significantly reduce food waste.

Dining Out without Compromise (Tips included)

Eating out doesn't have to be a challenge when following the renal diet. Here are some tips to navigate restaurant menus and make healthy choices:

- Research Restaurants: Many restaurants offer online menus, allowing you to browse options beforehand and identify renal-friendly choices.

- Ask Questions: Don't hesitate to ask questions about ingredients and preparation methods.

- Focus on Protein Sources: Choose grilled, baked, or poached lean protein options like fish, chicken, or turkey.

- Be Mindful of Sauces and Seasonings: These often contain high levels of sodium. Opt for dishes with light sauces or request sauces on the side.

- Control Portions: Restaurant portions are often much larger than recommended serving sizes. Consider sharing a plate or ask for a to-go box to portion out half for another meal.

- Bring Healthy Extras: Pack a side salad with low sodium dressing, fruit, or unsweetened applesauce to complement your meal.

Tips for Specific Restaurant Types:

- Fast Food: Opt for grilled chicken sandwiches without mayo, salads with low-sodium dressing on the side, or fruit cups for dessert.

- Italian Restaurants: Choose grilled or baked fish dishes, pasta with marinara sauce (avoid creamy sauces), or minestrone soup (watch out for added sodium).

- Mexican Restaurants: Go for grilled fish tacos, fajitas with lean protein and minimal sauce, or black bean soup.

Travel & Special Occasions: Adapting Your Diet (Tips included)

Maintaining a healthy renal diet while traveling or during special occasions requires some planning and flexibility. Here are some tips to navigate these situations:

Travel:

• Pack Snacks: Pack pre-portioned, renal-friendly snacks like nuts, dried fruit, or baby carrots with lowsodium hummus to avoid unhealthy choices on the road.

• Research Accommodation Options: Consider staying in accommodations with a kitchenette or kitchen facilities, allowing you to prepare some of your own meals.

• Explore Local Grocery Stores: Stock up on renal friendly staples and fruits upon arrival at your destination.

• Ask About Menu Options: When dining out, inquire about ingredients and preparation methods. Don't hesitate to request modifications to suit your dietary needs.

Special Occasions:

- Communicate with Your Host: Talk to the person hosting the special occasion beforehand. Explain your dietary restrictions and inquire about menu options. Offer to bring a dish you can enjoy to share with others.

- Focus on Enjoying the Company: While maintaining a healthy diet is important, prioritize enjoying the company and festivities. An occasional minor indulgence won't stop you from moving forward.

- Portion Control: Even at celebratory meals, practice mindful portion control. Focus on savoring smaller amounts of your favorite dishes.

Additional Tips for Travel and Special Occasions:

- Stay Hydrated: It's important to stay hydrated, especially when traveling. This helps flush out toxins and prevents dehydration.

- Be Flexible: Unexpected situations may arise. Embrace flexibility and focus on making healthy choices whenever possible.
- Maintain Your Medication Routine: Don't forget to Pack your medications and stick to your prescribed medication schedule.

Conclusion:

Living with the renal diet can be a positive and empowering experience. By understanding the benefits, planning your meals, making smart shopping choices, and adapting your diet during travel or special occasions, you can enjoy delicious, nutritious meals and maintain good kidney health for a long and fulfilling life. Remember, consult your doctor or registered dietitian for personalized guidance and support on your renal health journey.

BONUS

2024 Update on the Renal Diet: Emerging Trends and Research

The renal diet continues to be a cornerstone of managing chronic kidney disease (CKD). Here's a glimpse into some exciting trends and research advancements in 2024:

1.   **Focus on Personalized Nutrition:** A one-size-fits-all approach to the renal diet is gradually giving way to personalized plans. This considers factors like individual needs, disease progression, and overall health.

2.   **The Gut Micro biome and Kidney Health:** Research suggests a potential link between gut bacteria and kidney function. Studies are exploring how modifying the gut micro biome through prebiotics and probiotics might benefit kidney health.

3.   **Role of Plant-Based Protein Sources:** Plant-based protein sources like lentils, beans, and tofu are gaining

increased attention. They offer valuable protein while often being lower in phosphorus compared to animal protein sources.

4. **Technological Advancements:** Mobile apps and online platforms are evolving to provide personalized meal planning tools, recipe suggestions, and educational resources specifically tailored for the renal diet.

5. **Telehealth and Remote Support:** The rise of telehealth consultations allows for easier access to registered dietitians and healthcare professionals who can provide ongoing support and guidance on managing the renal diet.

Emerging Research on the Renal Diet: Exploring Dietary Patterns, Inflammation, and Nutrients

The landscape of the renal diet is constantly evolving, with exciting research exploring the impact of specific dietary patterns, inflammation management, and the potential benefits of certain nutrients on kidney function. Here's a deeper dive into these areas:

1. Impact of Specific Dietary Patterns:

Mediterranean Diet: Studies suggest the Mediterranean diet, rich in fruits, vegetables, whole grains, fish, and healthy fats, may be beneficial for kidney health. Its emphasis on plant-based foods and moderate protein intake aligns well with the renal diet's core principles. Research indicates the Mediterranean diet may help slow the progression of chronic kidney disease (CKD) and reduce inflammation.

DASH Diet: The DASH (Dietary Approaches to Stop Hypertension) diet emphasizes fruits, vegetables, low-fat dairy products, and whole grains while limiting red meat, saturated fat, and added sugars. This dietary pattern has been linked to lower blood pressure and a possible reduction in the risk of developing CKD.

2. Role of Inflammation and Dietary Modifications:

Chronic inflammation is increasingly recognized as a contributing factor to CKD progression. Certain dietary modifications may help manage inflammation and improve kidney health:

- Limiting Saturated Fats and Processed Foods: These can contribute to inflammation. Opting for healthier fats like olive oil and fish may be beneficial.

- Increasing Fruits and Vegetables: These are rich in antioxidants with anti-inflammatory properties.

- Including Whole Grains: Whole grains offer fiber, which can help regulate inflammation.

- Considering Omega-3 Fatty Acids: Found in fatty fish like salmon, omega-3s possess anti-inflammatory properties.

3. Exploring Potential Benefits of Specific Nutrients:

- Antioxidants: Antioxidants found in fruits, vegetables, and whole grains may help reduce oxidative stress and inflammation, potentially slowing CKD progression.

- Omega-3 Fatty Acids: As mentioned above, omega3s from fatty fish may have anti-inflammatory effects and offer cardiovascular benefits, crucial for people with CKD.

Important Note:

While these research areas are promising, it's essential to consult with your doctor or a registered dietitian before making significant dietary changes. Individual needs and CKD severity can influence the recommended dietary approach.

INCREDIBLE 60 DAYS MEAL PLAN

Day	Breakfast	Lunch	Dinner	Snack(s)
1	Oatmeal with Nuts and Seeds	Tuna Salad Lettuce Wraps	Baked Salmon with Lemon Herb Crust and Roasted Asparagus	Apple Slices with Cinnamon Peanut Butter, Edamame with Sea Salt
2	Whole-Wheat Toast with Avocado and Sliced Tomato	Chicken Caesar Salad with Homemade Dressing	Turkey Chili with Brown Rice	Greek Yogurt with Berries and Sliced Almonds, Carrot Sticks with Hummus
3	Smoothie with Spinach, Banana, and Almond Milk	Veggie Wrap with Low-Fat Yogurt Ranch Dip	Vegetarian Stuffed Peppers with Quinoa	Cottage Cheese with Chopped Vegetables and Herbs, Homemade Trail Mix
4	Scrambled Eggs with Spinach and Mushrooms	Lentil Soup with Whole-Wheat Bread	Chicken Stir-Fry with Vegetables and Brown Rice	Rice Cakes with Avocado and Sliced Tomatoes, Hard-Boiled Eggs
5	Cottage Cheese Bowl with Berries and Nuts	Vegetarian Black Bean Burgers with Sweet Potato Fries	Baked Cod with Lemon Dill Sauce and Roasted	Bell Pepper Slices with Guacamole, Air-Popped Popcorn with

Day	Breakfast	Lunch	Dinner	Snack(s)
			Sprouts	Yeast
6	Whole-Wheat Pancakes with Apple Compote	Leftover Chicken Salad Sandwich on Whole-Wheat Bread	One-Pan Lemon Herb Salmon with Roasted Asparagus and Quinoa	Berry Chia Seed Pudding, Edamame with Sea Salt
7	Yogurt Parfait with Granola and Berries	Turkey and Vegetable Pita Pockets	Shrimp Scampi with Zucchini Noodles	Cottage Cheese with Chopped Vegetables and Herbs, Homemade Trail Mix
Day	Breakfast	Lunch	Dinner	Snack(s)
8	Scrambled Eggs with Spinach and Mushrooms	Tuna Salad Lettuce Wraps	Vegetarian Chili with Kidney Beans and Corn	Greek Yogurt with Berries and Sliced Almonds, Carrot Sticks with Hummus
9	Oatmeal with Nuts and Seeds	Chicken Caesar Salad with Homemade Dressing	Turkey Chili with Brown Rice	Apple Slices with Cinnamon Peanut Butter, Edamame with Sea Salt
10	Whole-Wheat Toast with Avocado and	Veggie Wrap with Low-Fat Yogurt Ranch Dip	Baked Salmon with Lemon Herb Crust	Cottage Cheese with Chopped Vegetables and Herbs,

Day	Breakfast	Lunch	Dinner	Snack(s)
	Sliced Tomato		Roasted Asparagus	Homemade Trail Mix
11	Smoothie with Spinach, Banana, and Almond Milk	Lentil Soup with Whole-Wheat Bread	Chicken Stir-Fry with Vegetables and Brown Rice	Rice Cakes with Avocado and Sliced Tomatoes, Hard-Boiled Eggs
12	Cottage Cheese Bowl with Berries and Nuts	Vegetarian Black Bean Burgers with Sweet Potato Fries	Baked Cod with Lemon Dill Sauce and Roasted Brussels Sprouts	Bell Pepper Slices with Guacamole, Air-Popped Popcorn with Nutritional Yeast
13	Whole-Wheat Pancakes with Apple Compote	Leftover Chicken Salad Sandwich on Whole-Wheat Bread	Shrimp Scampi with Zucchini Noodles	Berry Chia Seed Pudding, Edamame with Sea Salt
14	Yogurt Parfait with Granola and Berries	Turkey and Vegetable Pita Pockets	One-Pan Lemon Herb Salmon with Roasted Asparagus and Quinoa	Cottage Cheese with Chopped Vegetables and Herbs, Homemade Trail Mix

15	Oatmeal with Nuts and Seeds	Tuna Salad Lettuce Wraps	Baked Salmon with Lemon Herb Crust and Roasted Asparagus	Apple Slices with Cinnamon Peanut Butter, Edamame with Sea Salt
16	Whole-Wheat Toast with Avocado and Sliced Tomato	Chicken Caesar Salad with Homemade Dressing	Turkey Chili with Brown Rice	Greek Yogurt with Berries and Sliced Almonds, Carrot Sticks with Hummus
17	Smoothie with Spinach, Banana, and Almond Milk	Veggie Wrap with Low-Fat Yogurt Ranch Dip	Vegetarian Stuffed Peppers with Quinoa	Cottage Cheese with Chopped Vegetables and Herbs, Homemade Trail Mix
18	Scrambled Eggs with Spinach and Mushrooms	Lentil Soup with Whole-Wheat Bread	Chicken Stir-Fry with Vegetables and Brown Rice	Rice Cakes with Avocado and Sliced Tomatoes, Hard-Boiled Eggs
19	Cottage Cheese Bowl with Berries and Nuts	Vegetarian Black Bean Burgers with Sweet Potato Fries	Baked Cod with Lemon Dill Sauce and Roasted Brussels Sprouts	Bell Pepper Slices with Guacamole, Air-Popped Popcorn with

Day	Breakfast	Lunch	Dinner	Snack(s)
				Nutritional Yeast
20	Whole-Wheat Pancakes with Apple Compote	Leftover Chicken Salad Sandwich on Whole-Wheat Bread	One-Pan Lemon Herb Salmon with Roasted Asparagus and Quinoa	Berry Chia Seed Pudding, Edamame with Sea Salt
21	Yogurt Parfait with Granola and Berries	Turkey and Vegetable Pita Pockets	Shrimp Scampi with Zucchini Noodles	Cottage Cheese with Chopped Vegetables and Herbs, Homemade Trail Mix
Day	Breakfast	Lunch	Dinner	Snack(s)
22	Scrambled Eggs with Spinach and Mushrooms	Tuna Salad Lettuce Wraps	Vegetarian Chili with Kidney Beans and Corn	Greek Yogurt with Berries and Sliced Almonds, Carrot Sticks with Hummus
23	Oatmeal with Nuts and Seeds	Chicken Caesar Salad with Homemade Dressing	Baked Salmon with Lemon Herb Crust and Roasted Asparagus	Apple Slices with Cinnamon Peanut Butter, Edamame with Sea Salt
24	Whole-Wheat Toast with Avocado and	Veggie Wrap with Low-Fat	Turkey Chili with Brown Rice	Cottage Cheese with Chopped Vegetables and

Day	Breakfast	Lunch	Dinner	Snack(s)
	Sliced Tomato	Yogurt Ranch Dip		Herbs, Homemade Trail Mix
25	Smoothie with Spinach, Banana, and Almond Milk	Lentil Soup with Whole-Wheat Bread	Chicken Stir-Fry with Vegetables and Brown Rice	Rice Cakes with Avocado and Sliced Tomatoes, Hard-Boiled Eggs
26	Cottage Cheese Bowl with Berries and Nuts	Vegetarian Black Bean Burgers with Sweet Potato Fries	Baked Cod with Lemon Dill Sauce and Roasted Brussels Sprouts	Bell Pepper Slices with Guacamole, Air-Popped Popcorn with Nutritional Yeast
27	Whole-Wheat Pancakes with Apple Compote	Leftover Chicken Salad Sandwich on Whole-Wheat Bread	Shrimp Scampi with Zucchini Noodles	Berry Chia Seed Pudding, Edamame with Sea Salt
28	Yogurt Parfait with Granola and Berries	Turkey and Vegetable Pita Pockets	One-Pan Lemon Herb Salmon with Roasted Asparagus and Quinoa	Cottage Cheese with Chopped Vegetables and Herbs, Homemade Trail Mix
Day	Breakfast	Lunch	Dinner	Snack(s)

29	Breakfast Burrito with Black Beans and Scrambled Eggs	Vegetarian Lentil Soup with Crusty Bread	Chicken Fajitas with Whole-Wheat Tortillas	Apple Slices with Cinnamon Peanut Butter, Air-Popped Popcorn with Nutritional Yeast
30	Scrambled Eggs with Spinach and Mushrooms (Week 1)	Tuna Salad Lettuce Wraps (Week 1)	Vegetarian Chili with Kidney Beans and Corn (Week 2)	Cottage Cheese with Chopped Vegetables and Herbs (Week 1), Carrot Sticks with Hummus (Week 1)
31	Whole-Wheat Toast with Avocado and Sliced Tomato (Week 1)	Chicken Caesar Salad with Homemade Dressing (Week 1)	Turkey Chili with Brown Rice (Week 1)	Greek Yogurt with Berries and Sliced Almonds (Week 1), Homemade Trail Mix (Week 1)
32	Smoothie with Spinach, Banana, and Almond Milk (Week 1)	Veggie Wrap with Low-Fat Yogurt Ranch Dip (Week 1)	Baked Salmon with Lemon Herb Crust and Roasted Asparagus (Week 1)	Rice Cakes with Avocado and Sliced Tomatoes (Week 1), Hard-Boiled Eggs (Week 1)

33	Cottage Cheese Bowl with Berries and Nuts (Week 1)	Leftover Chicken Salad Sandwich on Whole-Wheat Bread (Week 1)	One-Pan Lemon Herb Salmon with Roasted Asparagus and Quinoa (Week 2)	Bell Pepper Slices with Guacamole (Week 1)
34	Whole-Wheat Pancakes with Apple Compote (Week 1)	Turkey and Vegetable Pita Pockets (Week 1)	Shrimp Scampi with Zucchini Noodles (Week 1)	Berry Chia Seed Pudding (Week 1)
35	Yogurt Parfait with Granola and Berries (Week 1)	Vegetarian Black Bean Burgers with Sweet Potato Fries (Week 1)	Lentil Soup with Whole-Wheat Bread (Week 1)	Edamame with Sea Salt (Week 1)

DAY 36-60

(Continue rotating favorites or explore entirely new recipes).

Made in the USA
Coppell, TX
08 September 2024